Robert Vander Molen

THE
invisible
LOST BOOK
of
deep ocean fish

A ZEITGEIST PUBLICATION

SECOND EDITION

first printing

———

Acknowledgments

A number of the poems in this book appeared originally in *Alkahest, Collage, Mimeo, Poltergeist, Red Cedar Review,* and *Zeitgeist.* "Bow-Hunting" copyright © 1968 by Wesleyan University.

EDITOR'S PREFACE TO THE SECOND EDITION

Many a poet and many a book have come and gone
since the first edition of *The Lost Book* was pub-
lished in 1968. Many a delusion and hysteria have
settled over the national consciousness. Such pri-
ate lives and emotions as remain are tucked away in
corners where the television poets have not yet
reached.

So let it be. The weather is exceptionally
nice along the Lake Michigan coast today, and *The
Lost Book* has never seemed a better book than it
does now. It needed to be reprinted; it has been
changed somewhat, but it is still the same book, and
it shows the same genius. In another time, it might
have done better than it has--but this is the only
time we've got, and it has done well enough.

Poetry is, after all, not a business so much as
it is an awakening from a dream . . . in which "no
one speaks / And in a walking crowd / No one looks
to the side."

--Gary Groat
Saugatuck
May 21, 1970

CONTENTS

* * * * * * *

DECLARATION

I'm sleeping with your girl

Mankind

FIGURATIONS

Setting

1.

The streetcleaner   armored car
Stops around the 7 am corner
Of the curving curb   the driver
From his height
Pulls a cigarette

I have coffee
And my enlarging   sense of sound
On the steps
I smooth over my teeth
With my tongue

With a pure thought
Of standing in a hall
With oak doors

2.

In the afternoon
The sun pours on the floor
And warms my feet
        The breeze twists
The round handle   dangling
Of the window shade
        The nuance of heat
From the pavement
Mostly   stays low

The taste of blood today
As the day before
As just as foolish
        With awkward teeth
And cigarettes

Inch-worms in the trees
Just above silence
Eat holes in darkness

I.

In my borrowed car
And early rain   interseason
In familiar march or sooner
With rivets on a brisk
Windshield
And my arm   hanging open
Driving south with a woman
Seated with hemorrhage
Like my mother on a dock
Pregnant
With the sun glancing sheaths
Off the water

I put a blanket
Beneath her

Yet from her house
I swallowed much time
Looking into the yard
From inside windows
          Although I confuse
Particulars   with color

Toes of wind
From breaking night clouds
Fill me with photographs
Of the seasons

And I nod in the direction
Of fixing dreams

She was a child
Of a woman
With good breasts
Veined in the bath
With soap

Wore a small leather coat
That she took off

At night
Her men hammer
My head with fence boards
In settings   of no walls
And no horizons
        They say quietly
There are no surface excuses
Inside of the round plunging plane

She dances nudely
In vague time

This is a mistake

I sit in Kollens Park
For that ferry
Too early to dock   in whitewash
        On a side trip
        Old enough not to be lonely
Like bouquet wallpaper
Faded
In my mind
With shirts hanging
Behind a door
        With a brass headboard

And over the bed   stories
Of dirt farm roads

There was a brick path
Around to the rear of the house
Stolen   from the Depression
With vermilion ricochets
Under the shrubs and pointed grass
Baked in the sun
        And with damp feet
I peek into the kitchen
And watch her with coffee
And touch her earrings
In loose black hair

II.

1.

In San Francisco
The fog hoods in
Over the stucco rise
And eastward
        And so on south
And sea lions   rasp
In black rocks
In gray sand
In sky flying boulders

On a cliff
Where I slept
Turning to keep warm
On a shallow patch
In daytime yellow
And orange brush   wiry
        The ocean was speaking
Drawing bodies
        And the curt wind
Crackled
With the forward wave

During day
Bird white   spilled
On the outer sea rocks
        Hot   very hot
And on the turning coast highway
Rumbling   buses
With whole fuckloads   of kids

I spotted a woman
In a polka dot dress
Gliding a car
Who would sit   watching
A boy push a sailboat
With one side of her face
In the leaf-edge movements
Of a city pond   as part
Of a painting
In bedrooms   for the 1950s
With a purse slung
From the shoulder

2.

I had an old friend
Who went insane
With whom I dabbled in thought
When he was then
Blondheaded
When we traced breezes
From one sun
        Our feet stained black
In the black lake sun

He can't remember my dreams
And my imagination
        Of broken bottles in ferns
Below the park   and green mirrors
        He only begs

3.

Another woman
Endorsed by hikers
Picked me up
In the Sur forest
Divided by tourists

Bought me sauterne
And stopped much later
When I was sleeping
At
A reservoir
With olive like trees
In dust
And dwarfish deer
Towards dark

She talked about sex
        Was a grandmother

She said
Home is where the sex
Is

                    III.

1.

Lively eyes
Prod
My face
With sea crabs
        Grip
My clothes
And empty me out
On a Seattle dock

I walk up the steps
To my room
Where the girls bring customers
        I'm the only one
Who holds his bed
All night

        They brush my hand

        I want to kiss
Necks

The blind chinese woman
At the desk
Has a little partner
In black glasses
        She talks
A lot
He doesn't

They go away

2.

White-yellow
Jellyfish
A few inches
Below surface waves
        I dump wine
On their heads
From the ferry

Thinking: I'm
Going farther   and farther

And the wind   whips
My hair
Very majestically
        I should stand
Bare
In the prow
And bend my hips
Back

THE STATE OF

Being desperate
Is something like madness

An issue holding apart
Walls

And the fury leaks away
With retarded purposes

Like the brown grocery bag
Under my window

POSITION #32

Position #32
She said
And I grunted
Beginning to dream
Of a stagecoach   and me
Wearing black   to my toes
        She said I couldn't tell her
        I said   fine

DIARY OF A FRIEND

I.

It was all finished
When I was out of nerves
Couldn't read
        I sat up with Bill
Playing songs
        (First I began
Sitting in the backyard
On the bamboo chairs
        Sick of weaklings)
        Didn't hardly see you
And I moved out
Of town

II.

Frondescent trails
And the river shrunk
        You got your earrings in the mail
Without a stamp
        I got high on pills and sat
Under a tree like a Buddha
And things got silent

Fourth of July

III.

Hearing from the family
Where was I?
And Uncle Floyd
Died
When they took out his lungs

He had a fondness for firecrackers

I STAND IN MY WINDOW

I stand in my window
In the configurations of light
Rebounding walls
When my tree was swinging leaves
I'd shower and fix bacon
And wear an old shirt

She lies in the shade of my bed
        Summer eschewed
            Lying with legs around poems

And all the photographs I took
Of you then you
Then you
But my camera was stolen

At night I ran my hands
Over wooden sculptures
At the art center

Walked with a closed coat

ROBIN

She would never step out of her clothes
And dance to the bed
She was too sensitive
        Also   she cried
About dead animals

OURS

Our pasts
Are dissonant
A Korean latrine today
    My potted plant
Stolen for the window
Holds tight
Against the screen
    The woman standing
In the street
Is a Gauguin dress
Flinging across a pineal garden
    Sadder
When you peer closer
To the skin

SAW YOU

Saw you 3 times today
I wrote
Consumed with
Startling
Older and less
Full breasted

LAKE MICHIGAN

To begin with
The lake gets bluer
Then black

WHALES

High along the lake
Whales were buried
Frozen
The musk buffets
In the trees
And the heat coming down
Walks barefoot
On the shaded burrs
Along the boardwalk

SOULS

I am one of the old Chinese
Who soothes his soul
In the rock etchings   in the leaves
        I am rich
A warlord of the mountains
        I have many dogs
And they shake to their toes when they bark

PURPOSE

        The poet
        Observes
        Changes in the chemical
        Tempo
        Of everyday

        He thinks,
                I would
                Like to stop
                Writing
                And find a wife
                And have a few children

IN THE AFTERNOON

I.

Groups speaking about the war
All very tightly interwoven

Sparks in their eyes (eye)
They don't like it

Something like the bomb
People have neglected to remember

They have to plan of course
And it's a habit

II.

Walking across the grass
I hasten to lie in bed with novels

And the girl there
Spraying herself in the sun

Blank eyes on the yellow blanket
Her legs opened to cool

III.

There is a fire downtown today
But no one is going to see it

A whole block is burning downtown today
From the corner Army Surplus store

JUSTINE

She moved here because she was a dancer
From Toledo with her trunk
And there are many jobs here
For costumed starry dancers
        And found a one-woman apartment
Out in Oak Woods
A year ago or so

She is a hetero-bag of faces
And movements
And deluded walls move
Like children screaming with poisoned ears
        She is midnight
A shadow of streets and walls
A hooded inquisition in the minds of owls

Established well
Real truths are found in her apartment
She has whispered

BIG SABLE RIVER

When I was sick in the spring
I went north   camping
Up along the shore
Counting waves
The snow fences still   dug in

We pulled back in the irregular hollows
        Père Marquette died here
And was exhumed later
        We nailed down a tent
And the hills were quiet
And sand cold   on the water
Leveled   dammed at Hamlin
Ice shelves in the morning

Honkers broke off the water
Wound up the pine hill dunes
To the faceless birches
        Winter ate at roots
        We didn't spy any deer
On the shores

The town washed away
And changed the river
        A sign opens   old time
Metal cellars
Above the sound of water
Washing through low grass

Climbing budded hills
Around the backwater
Catching the acres of reflected leaves
On the rolling
Descending floors
        Their color sucked up
In the snow   now silver

The highest I could walk
Always faced me
With the fleshy backside
Of the following hill

STORM

Thunder and thunder
When young boys watch the sky
Lying in bed
        Wiping the horizon
Now light
            The rain sprays off walls
Fills the grass
        The poplar that crackled leaves
In the afternoon
Is silent
        The home that walked
In the snow
Suffers in the rain
        And two people
Stand
Inhaling gasoline
            Oh but the white magic power
Of lightning
        Where lightning pierces like metal
And showers in sparks

MUSIC

Too cold to get out of bed
That is too narrow
When your girl was up and gone
Early
When romance is as dirty rusty
As the railyard
        Oh there are many equals
Looking at the whole
Sliced between sliding glass doors
And slow music

THE ATTIC

Living as you do
Is like a calendar for the righteous
Who knows what happens
In your attic
With the brown log cabin ceiling

Oh it's nice when it's raining
And if you have a fan
For the summer

        In one corner
Is a pioneer desk
And in another
Your two glaring cats

And on your stairs
Coast footsteps
Envelopes and old letters

PLAIN-CLOTHES MEN

Plain-clothes men
Sit in two cars
With hands
For maps
    And in the window
Fall rains
Long Seattle rains
Where a boy
Ticks his feet
On the wall
    When the rain stops
Long enough
For a breeze
The leaves clutter the air
Like dusk
Building layer and layer

PAUL FROM THE RAILYARD

The little Mexican
Was on a permanent payroll
Lived in a heated boxcar
With furniture   on a side track
Where the coal ramparts used to rise up
    Had troubles with his young wife
And sprinkled   flour on the floor
To catch a man's track

Was glad to be working

I.

1.

This is summer
When weeds bore into cement block foundations
Katydids
And sitting
        A younger woman shrieks
With laughter
On the small porch below my window
        The front lawn tree
Covers me from sunlight
        Anthills cozy up to roots
In shade
        In shade
The early calls
From black ripened trees
        Squirrel trees
And tattered child books
        And the basking
Dry-all sun
        Board fences
Musky
With attic-old studs
Blackened and blackened

This is summer
Summer's improvisations
But surprises that are no longer surprises
        Green and hay
        Backyard raspberries
From old city stalks
        And pawing dogs at twilight

Sometimes bullet rains
And large sharp splattering impressions
        Bullet rains
And the loneliness of drugs
Lost afternoons between humming fans
Tarnished gold fixtures
And varnished sills

With my hands under my chin
I watch the street
For friends
        Around
My propped stick window

2.

In the attic I can remember
The remains of families
I never knew
        Put together photographs I never studied
        As a child
As a child
        The drinking glasses and beads
Baby cheeks and hats

        But my face changes
In the iron flower mirror
In the humid mattress
        I sniff the trees
Where they billow

II.

Secured in the body
In the cells of wood
        Roving eyes
I hear him
In the stepping grass
Blocks away
        The trucks on the avenue
Thunder through my bed

Car doors closing
        Miles away
Miles away
        With nothing I can do

Breezes
Hanging in passive
Sight alertness
        This is summer
This   colored odors
Effervescent snapshot odors

Myself smoothly instated
And no fear
What to fear?

And a small white moth
Slips into air
Darts
In its own light

CADENCE

Women who don't talk
Are golden shadows
Moving about
Moving

But this is a myth
Like Lee in jail
Like Robert
In the hospital
For stealing cars
From work to drive
To New York

A combination of characters
        We know women
        We create women

Lee copied Robert
For years
In the way he talked
And moved
        But Robert just
Went crazy
Said Lee
        And Lee walked away
From the army

We drank
In a church-yard
In my dreams
Listening to Robert
        Made women shadows
On the brick walls

LIVING

Ladybugs gather to driftwood
At the ripple hard beach

Corn tassels
Shatter in the ragged field

The sun blinks
And crawls south

The winter killed my great grandmother
With the gray braid
        If she could have lived until spring
My father said
She would have lived

FISHING WITH JAKE

The water dropped steep   right away
A few feet from shore
On the end of the stubby dock
        Fireflies invisible
In the morning with drapes still pulled
And cars   in drives
Where he rented the water   south of Holland
        Cottages
And in the lake a fishermen gas station
Where we stop .   before running the channel
        The sun risen across state
And Jake having called the weather station
At the coast guard base
Stares out to sea with his hand on the motor

FIRST PERSON

I.

You are nothing contradictory
Or unreal
Smoking cigarettes   nude
With your curtains dyed green

So dark as chestnuts

A sprinkle   of brooding oaks
In the alley   never
Ready for snow

II.

And you don't hesitate
While I wear my smile
Leaning a smaller face

I listen to you
Retract: squirrels
With mouth pockets
        A slow fisherman
Miles north

But your legs don't fool me
Nor the shadows
        Nor the newspapers

I like to fish
And in the fall
The fish bite at leaves
Falling

III.

And if it floods tonight: good
I am round
I feel real again   making
It
I'll go back to Seattle

CAUGHT BLOODLESS

Ice on Lake Michigan   a refractory
Of green lights
Several stories   deep
        They spear   black sharp
Sturgeon   and you hold an invisible
Lost book of deep ocean fish
Whose eyes protract for the slightest
Echo   of light under pressure
        Your eyes are dull
Green eyes
        And under sail   boats
With sparks racing   rails intersecting
To cut   even fingers
Lying bunched on unmoved snow

GIRL AND HER YELLOW DOG

A fire in the sand
Smolders
Wisping in dead rocks
And the desertion
Of a warm morning
Is silent fall
But the gulls
Squawk in a sudden---
Along the brown picket snow fence
And the sun smolders

BACKWARD

The night breeze
Is a woman   who turns and turns
Her feet in her sleep
Who rolls towards the wall
        And rolls back
With her arms held close to her side

LATE OCTOBER

Winter clouds tumbled
South
From the arctic

And people on the walk
Scattered
With the first rough drops
Of rain

In the restaurant
Men
Watched the windows
For snow
Their coffees
Turning cold

TIRED

Dead tired
Black Georgia tired
And we dragged our tired feet
Past the fresh sign to Andersonville

Are earthquakes weather?
Don'ts---the rain of anti-anti's

GAS MISTAKE

The explosion started like a
Dog in the cans
In the violent grove
We saw the rudiments of our mind hesitate

Stopped like the dream
Moment of death
We stood precariously
And then could never remember exactly

PAPERS

Papers twist
And attack trees
And the ground is emerald smiles

And the stick pedestrians
Over there
Hold on to their souls

The old leaves are
Dried red soldiers

FILLED
(for Ezra Pound)

Filled with ambrosia
I lost my pact with such and such

SUNGLASSES

From a dim green Wizard of Oz falling
She walks and affixes
Sunglasses
From brick
And quarter stale pictures
     But the windows breathe for air
In regular absorbed eyes

Sometimes an indefinable bird
Flies up there
Above the motif
Stretching legs
That lengthen and withdraw

And it is all dull and weary
But I don't think she knows
Walking where she walks
There is a lot on her mind
Between the long-up cement walls

DRUNK

I'm drunk
Again tonight
And
The same is not the same
And the trees have dropped their veiny leaves
    I have covered the leaves extensively
Before

JIM

The hours
Mumbling with the broken leaves
Across the ringed and swaying street

The deepening park
Across there
Beyond to the parkers
The tracks beyond there
To the glowing city
And all swept up from the north
In leaves

Today
Too many cigarettes
And coffees

THE BROWN COAT

Stare when you've seen her
Wear that brown coat
That by now is a museum piece
        Tracking the late snow
And the hill trees shake down
To the park
        With the felt collar
In a sleeping wind
And drifting hair

ABOVE THE SMOOTH HILL

When things run forever
She would hold me
And look to the city where we stood

I looked
And quiet in the kettle drum forest

I looked
And she danced and kissed the trees
And her truths ran forever

NORTH-EAST OF NEWBERRY

I.

The forest is Hawthorne
Black mass
Moody
        Not flat
But difficult
To discern
Levels
While walking

The logging road
Is a closing down green
To the interior

Sit on a stump
Barkless and smooth
Afraid to turn your back

Turn into clearings
Like eyes

Somewhere two beech trees
Rub together
From an accident
Screeching wildcats

Occasional spring pools
Of water without fish

II.

Deer stepping
With sharp brittle legs
In the grass
Waving towards the edge
Of a ravine
        A sudden snap
Pulls their ears
For a raccoon with three legs
Followed by offspring
Who tunnel into the grass
Which rolls like river seaweed

III.

Deer stepping in the stumps
Of the tooth pick mill
40 years dying
        The edge of the ravine
A slipping buoyancy
Of sawdust

They scatter into the forest
Into a shield of leaves
On a width of 6 inch paths
That follow into the swamps

IV.

The only protection
Into the trees
Are the contours
        Deepened in rain

Levels and levels
And rotten bear stumps

And quietness of leaves

Inverted directions
And leaf dust

JUNE

The white bed
In a season of horrors
        I pick your bra
From the carpet
And drape it over the headboard

BAYONNE

Bayonne
Escaped from the Basques
        A thick peninsula
Coming out of New York
On my vision
Of a ride
From the median
Hugging out of the Holland Tunnel
        Where I stopped with the driver
In little neighborhood bars
His mania   my pleasure
His crawling into Pennsylvania
And my forgetting of time principle
Of schedule   of back to Michigan
In falling fall   still sweating in the east
On peeled streets
American old
But some time since it was tossed out
Of thinking

LEE

        Me and my girl
        Would like to buy a farm
        With wooded acres and a stream
        For midnight swims in the moon
                We talk about it
        While it rains
                And I know I'm not making it

                And how ever hard we try
        We aren't satisfied

DISPLACEMENT

The tremor
Of death   holding
Rough holes
        Cracks in the street
        Splits in the hills

A chisel

Or steps
Into the garage

A woman
Burning in a tree
        And a charred stump
Where the hound
Sniffs
At part· of a dress
In the ashes

FALL AFFAIR

Streets polished   flat black
And nursery verse
Geese   flying wedges
And apartment women   wrapped
In their own linen   ears awake

All-day scatterings   of orchards
Falling   the breeze blowing
From the country   and out

Streams of tissue   trees
And evening   opening legs
And solitary dancing
No smoke
No anger

STREETLIGHT

The empathic streetlight
Swings
And swings
And balls a shadow
Larger than windows

BACK AGAIN

It's so warm   the sky
Burning away gum wrappers
And you on my bed
Thinking vacation
     Cigarette in my scented hand
     Thinking jokes
     Down one more street
     We should lie outside

Leaves hobble
Back and forth in the street
When the soil melts
With animal teeth

SALMON AND SEAWEED

The smell of salmon wind
Digs into the hill and rakes the grass
As it works up   bends
The sprouts of flowers
Along the trees

But I can smell the pollen in the ground
As it beats the soil   the colors
Full of grace
For children

And seaweed in the rocks
Cold and harmless   undulate
Where the lake bounces
Down the shore

FOR YOU

After your love   covered with dew
Swift so-called fire
With you   awake
I think   with your eyes through
The ceiling
Seeing   meshes of wires
In night sounds
I roll around   fighting elbows
I remember certain half times
But again   that's your mind
And your sweat

YOU AGAIN

Since changing months
That ride over hills
Into towns   with green southern squares
And bells ringing   whitely
      A bed without lights
And my jacket on the chair

Oh I carry my bag
In sleep
And meet you
While the wind turns to battering

And in the morning we sit   and smoke
      Listening to Dvorak
With time   a fragrant chasm
Of drugs
      But no one speaks
And in a walking crowd
No one looks to the side

TRANSIENT SUN

Transient sun in the clouds
In the lake
Across the far elk shore
      The children talk about
The Indian treasure   Chief Wabasis
In the muck woods
Overturned in the spring
      They talk down about the docks
Where the outboards   tie up
All aluminum
And gasoline   disquieting
Sprinkles the water

          PIECES OF CANOPY

1.

Rain in the empty trees
And buds drop
Shucks on the aging walk

2.

In the day
The sun boils
The down-sloping sand from the hill
Where flies cast circles
On stagnant
Alewives

3.

Rain is a peaceful agent
A fixation of disintegrated heats

I watch the flashing fists

Coaxing a fire
That forgets to tremble

4.

And later
Plummeting
Through singing trees
And plucking white fruit blossoms

5.

In February
I liked to read by the window
With a rug over my bare feet
        Watched for snow

In April
I gave up writing

VACATION

The puddles are droning
From here miles to Lake Michigan
In the black and white day
        A cigarette
While the water pricks
        Made love
Almost sacredly with Cathy
And the Siamese cats crept
Along the shelf and across the refrigerator
        While the others are gone
I stare from the pale windows
Touch the dripping
        Cathy loves me
Sits quietly
In the air

INCIDENT ABOVE THE LAKE

The sand kicks the surface
When the woman
Walks   hugging a woman shadow
After the year that the toads
Were so numerous

Jointed leaves
Of the sumac
Are dyed   old red
In places
Around the sand

And swung windows of the cabins
Creased with rain
Bang at her hands
Saying   "cunt cunt cunt . . ."

THE THIN WINDOWS

The thin windows are my eyes
I've taped a red cut-out
Picture of a man running
On the plaster wall above our bed

She is here too

Her cut hair lies glued to water
In the heavy sink

Twilight separates the room
I see her face when I close my eyes

Her plant died when I opened the window
One day   it sits in the kitchen
Dropped leaves cover the earth

IN WESTERN MICHIGAN

A pale dog found us
Nude   atop
The rise from the beach
Up the banked sand
Glued   from winter
In shade   on the wrong slant
     Logs tossed
Nosefirst   everyway

Where it was already
Basting hot   in the morning
Figuring in the sand
In its hot reeds   beyond
The leaves

Had to run down to cool
My face   and you got
Sand in you

BOW-HUNTING

Went bow-hunting with my father
A few times when that was his interest
     Sitting on a stump in Newaygo
Getting a little sun in October
     Shot arrows in the sky
Smelling bonfires   crossing in the trees
Crossing mossy brooks
     This was all second growth
Twisted orchards some farmer lost in the woods
Only small ground apples
     Run down grassy ravines
No lakes left   but ferns
Tree bridges

FALL AND WINTER

Snow encloses my room
(I guess I'll stay here)
And the light on my far wall
Moves with the clouds
Without nerves

The identical trees are clotted
In the long sky
That changed yellow

(Leaves covered the pricks
Of grass
In the winter that raged
In the trees
And smashed field gray boulders)

Fix meals
And dream the dreams
That clutter
All my friends'
Nights
And mild days open my window

(The rain washed
On the streets ideally named
Changing this block
From that block)

Signs in upper windows
And pictures
In the peppered wind
And on the street
People change paths
In the afternoon

AT MARCIA'S HOUSE

Touching my hands on the table   which is cold
Dim morning   when the rain has stopped ticking
Because I love coffee and the silence of the mirror
Writing with yellow sun pencil when I please
      I look at the veins in my hands   while
The eaves dry

WINTER TIRES

Changed the tires on my car
Today
With my knees on the pebble drive
Left orange peelings on the brick wall
Said   fuck it
And got drunk afterwards
Watching the strange birds
Hopping trees
Making it up to Canada

THE POOL

Water is still in the pool
With green blue bottom
Shredded fronds irritate the surface
In the sun
I put fish one time in the feeding creek
A shaded inlet facing the mountains
I carried in separate pails from the southern lake
        The fish dart near the bottom
While I sit tossing twigs

DEEP IN LEAVES

Feet deep
In leaves

(The wind
Blew over the horizon
East)

In the evening
The sky
Doesn't move

Hands in your
Pockets
        A penis
Of crumbled leaves

INDOORS

When you were sick
With my baby
I stayed indoors   all day
And you had the drapes pulled
      I chewed gum

And I drank beer
And thought about my early church
With decades of gum   under benches
And narrow windows
And candles on holidays

Could see your green bushes
From the vent of one window
And leaves which were in the sun
Not moving but lush
      A warm day

      You muggy son of a bitch
You said

And you talked in Spanish   sometimes
In a light drug sleep

MY STREET

Nobody drives down my street in the morning
No rustle of gravel to the curbs
I think   as quiet as wishing

My darling who runs in my dreams
Whom I no longer know   not even her breasts
Although they fill pockets in her bulky shirt

The knots in the tree are your eyes

IN CALIFORNIA

In California I meet with her
And we part history
Her with her crazy family
And debts
I with my romance

YOU WITH THE RED BEDSPREAD

Slept under your red bedspread
With vase on the dresser
With lilacs   played nurse
When you were with the flu
Fixing your coffee with sugar
And cream   stared at
My nose in your coffee
And caressed silence

A LETTER

A letter
To you
My single lover
On a world that circulates
Too daringly

A letter
To spend something

A slip of the senses
From a green view

A letter to you
(your name has slipped)
A letter to write
With the phallus of my thoughts

TOGETHER

Together is different
Than apart and walking
Miles pressed upon planes of miles
To the apartment
And a few friends assembled there
When you reach the door

Together your eye thinks
Altogether different
And your limbs and the sense is different
Different than you had thought

THE THEATRE

The theatre
Closes
Summer stock for the 20th season
This falling season

Starlings flow across oiled grass this morning
Well adapted
After these years
The Ottawas are not here to trap them

The letters I receive
Will not return

TO DAVID

Lustrous sea
Or so it seems foaming through its brown sea teeth
I see you in a painting my friend has completed
Sometime ago

On the coast he is near
To watch Jeffers' gulls
Or to reply with hands in uniform pockets

Droplets smashed like the sea works
In the reach
Dissolving out of reach
Sometime ago when you painted

THE PARK

The park
Was larger at the turn of the century--I used
To remember as I walked
In the fair

Remember the crisp photographs--as I
Threaded like a snake through the brush
In the tall elms
Up the hill for raspberries

SILENCE

Silence
Is kind
        As pleasant
        As
A love
That we no longer
Sleep with
        But
        Dream of

CAN YOU GLUE EGGS TOGETHER, DARLING?

Can you glue eggs together, darling?
Glued in order that no separation can be observe
No loose pieces
No shells on the table
Perhaps you can tape
Only tape will be irregular
It can only fix on the equator
No, tape will not be possible.

EVERYONES WHORE

Everyones whore
Keeps you warm
But you miss your friends
In the winter
        You don't hear her speak
Because she doesn't
Yet the cat scampers
With icy toes around the floor
Won't go near the door
And died crawling up under the car

NATURE

The river floods
A woman laughs
And logs topple
Over the falls

THE MOUNTAIN

You have to climb steps
For six hours   to reach the hut
On the pine tree mountain with the difficult name
Above the trees   sighting long patches of forest
In the morning with coffee in hand
Fingering for a cigarette   and the air
Is stiffly thin
        Happy as the sun yet as distant
As Manfred and the chamois hunter
Climbing up for snow to melt in your palm
And you never see a bird   larger
Than the dust of hawks in the valley

SUDDEN SNOW

The snow higher
Than a cat's head
From the window

And the trees rock
In the smell of snow

Good day to drink
And hold a blanket

Footprints on the floor
On the tile
Lightly   hazing away

Good day to live
In the belly of a reindeer
And drink blood

SEPTEMBER

I.

After it turned cold
There was rain   up north it snowed
      In the afternoon I had a fever
Janey put me to bed
Gave me vitamins and juice
I fell asleep in wet skin
With bad dreams of childhood

II.

It was Indian Summer
That broke   full of command
A few days later   new shadows
      I was warm in the sun
Thinking of the Chicago Tribune picture
Of moon and Indians   and we
Tramped along the river
When she was dressed

WINTER

Factories breathe deeper
With winter
You can see from your mailbox
The cleats of snow scuffled
By sexless schoolmates
With white arms in sleeves
And so forth   the Monet sky
Crawls down the tops of streets
Reminding you of bed
And in snow dust windows
You margin your face in everyones eye

THE BRIDGE

The Pearl Street bridge
Holds hands
With darkness
        Where I used to drive
To work   unloading trucks
All night   drinking coffee
While the drivers tossed pennies
Drank beer behind the steel pillars
        My boss old and no teeth
Screwed girls in a buggy
One time   "let the horse
Just walk down the road"

The water trembles
Downstream
From the upriver rapids   in summer
I used to take my girl home
On my way back to work
She'd sneak up her back stairs
And I'd blink my lights
And leave

LOVE AND HATE

    Following one lover
    The next
    Who felt the hate of the last

THE SINK

                    The yellow
                    Sink
                    Hunching in that corner
                    Whispering
                    In that cracked
                    To the
                    Covered floor
                    Corner
                    Please
                    Sweet
                    My covered
                    Death
                    Whisper to another
                    Corner god

WINTER TOWN

A semi-round year has pulled itself
Now fastened as far as it can go
(Now fastened not to slip)
        The millennium of children in the waves
To yelling like the waves
Before the turned crab hulls
Before the sanded dolphin hooks

And now?
And together the sight fumbles
Down the running sand

The bells and I try to count by them
Over the white hills
To the winter town out of context
Someplace overloaded with time

MY MINISTER

My minister
Falls into
That story
Category
Novel
Example
For an instance
Red
        Red for
Your hair
And the passion
Surprised
So soon
Forgotten
I'm   I am sorry
        That's it
My minister
Thought my dreams
In haunted
My
Nightmares
He's a crook
Red
That's correct
That's it
Red
        Oh
And I
        Hope
I see
        Again Red
This fall
        You
And Red
Don't forget I do
Sensitize
To awakening
Oh Red
I do think of you

                              MELODY

A white cat and a nude wall
You sitting in the algerian shade

And the melody of a clock
Where it stood
In the room with dim rug
        Dusted table
Oh, how the old ladies
Hands
Pruned up

Then again,
The old man fixing his tackle
On sprinkled garden steps
        His pole in the tomato
Leaves and the beans

I remember lying with you
Your hair in my eyes
Your body tucked into my mind

When I watched your breathing back
I played in the dusty sun from our glassy ledge

The school busses when you dressed
And arranged your face in the mirror

I, silent as an armchair
I follow your perfume

And this is more or less a dream
Looking for footsteps
Green curtains and books
        Will the wind
Drive
Everything through the streets

                    I scratch my scalp
               Saying: oh yes,
               Everyone has all passed away

                         MY UNCLE

               My uncle
               Prince Henry the Navigator
               Never really got on a ship
               Very often

               In his life he promised
               To meet Prester John
               With his crusade
               Into Africa

                    Sat on his porch in Lisbon
               And dreamed about maps

                 *   *   *   *   *   *   *

                         East Lansing, Grand Rapids,
                         New York, Los Angeles,
                         San Francisco, Hingham.
                         1965-68

Zeitgeist Publications

#1   Ken Lawless, *The Fables*, Book I,
     Volume 1, SBN 87649-000-3
     (short satire) $1.00

#2   Robert Vander Molen, *Blood Ink*,
     SBN 87649-001-1 (poetry) $1.00

#3   Ken Lawless, *The Fables*, Book I,
     Volume 2, SBN 87649-002-X
     (short satire) $1.00

#4   Robert Vander Molen, *The Invisible
     Lost Book of Deep Ocean Fish*,
     SBN 87649-003-8 (poetry) $1.25

#5   A. Quinn Smith, *The Eighteenth Floor*,
     SBN 87649-004-6 (poetry) $1.25

#6   Greg Kuzma, *Something at Last Visible*,
     SBN 87649-005-4 (poetry) $1.25

#7   Ken Lawless, *Tailing Off*,
     SBN 87649-006-2 (poetry) $1.25

#8   Fred Rue Jacobs, *Every Woman is a
     Virgin Somewhere*, SBN 87649-007-0
     (drama) $1.50

#9   Paul Weinman, *My Sister's Underwear*,
     SBN 87649-008-9 (poetry) $1.50

#10 James Mechem, *Girls Will Be Girls*,
     SBN 87649-009-7 (short stories) $1.50

#11 Ken Lawless, *Amper-sand & Question-
     mark*, SBN 87649-010-0 (poetry) $1.50

#12 Raymond DiPalma, *Between the Shapes*,
     SBN 87649-011-9 (poetry) $1.50

#13 Judith Anne Greenberg, *Fire in August*,
     SBN 87649-015-1 (poetry) $1.50

#14 Robert M. Benn, *Confessions of Crystal
      Mike*, SBN 87649-012-7 (novel) $1.50

#15 Robert Vander Molen, *Variations*,
      SBN 87649-016-X (poetry) $1.25

#16 Ken Lawless, *Twenty Characters in
      Search of an Academic Novel*,
      SBN 87649-014-3 (poetry) $1.25

published by zeitgeist in may again
for all the lost things